BAHÍYYIH <u>KH</u>ÁNUM
THE GREATEST HOLY LEAF

_KH_ÁNUM
The Greatest Holy Leaf

as remembered
by

MARZIEH GAIL

GR

GEORGE RONALD
OXFORD

GEORGE RONALD, Publisher

Softcover Edition 1982

Softcover Edition
ISBN 0–85398–113–2

*Dedicated to the memory of my father and mother,
Ali-Kuli Khan, Nabílu'd-Dawlih, and Florence
Breed <u>Kh</u>ánum, who made it possible for me to enter
the presence of 'Abdu'l-Bahá, of <u>Kh</u>ánum, and of
Shoghi Effendi, Guardian of the Bahá'í Faith*

KHÁNUM

The Greatest Holy Leaf

KHÁNUM

The Greatest Holy Leaf

Her photograph, taken about 1895, shows a slim figure in Victorian dress – a narrow tailored jacket, with embroidered collar and cuffs, and buttoned down the front a spreading, floor-length skirt, with vertical flowered bands, the general effect being a delicately elegant blend of East and West. A kerchief, barely visible. She stands facing the camera, her hands loose at the sides, dark hair off the face and hanging down her back, the ears showing, the face fragile and delicate; under curving brows the long blue eyes gaze off into distance, and her presence is somehow diffident and regal at the same time.

This is Khánum, the Most Exalted Leaf, the Lady *par excellence*, the Liege Lady of the people of Bahá, and next to her brother 'Abdu'l-Bahá, 'the brightest embodiment of that love which is born of God . . .'[1]

She lived to be 'the last survivor of a glorious and heroic age',[2] and she has been gone now almost fifty years.

If you were ever in her presence you encountered the earliest hours of the Bahá'í Faith. You saw a being who, when she was two years old, had seen great Ṭáhirih, a guest then in the princely home of Bahá'u'lláh. You saw one whose family had, because they followed the Báb, been stripped of their fortune and station in a single day; one who had cowered, with her mother the Navváb, inside their pillaged house in Ṭihrán, dreading from moment to moment a message that would tell them: 'Bahá'u'lláh, Who was chained in the Black Pit, is no longer on this earth.'

At seven, she was banished with the other exiles from her homeland. Later on – at least after her Father returned from the wastes of Kurdistán, and there were those years when our young Faith prospered in Baghdád – she must have known some happiness, because, reminiscing, she seemed to take pleasure in recalling that city. But afterward came the further banishment to Constantinople and Adrianople, and a winter in the last-named town from which she never physically recovered, a terrible winter of poor housing and want, a time when the Faith seemed to have reached its lowest ebb.[3]

So, almost from the beginning of conscious-

ness, she had her share in the sorrows and bur-
dens of her Father, Bahá'u'lláh. When she was
only a teenager, He entrusted important missions to her, missions delicate and extremely
grave. As the years went by, He wrote that the
remembrance of her was like the fragrance of
musk, and He granted her a station 'such as
none other woman hath surpassed',[4] which
means that she ranked with long-dead heroines
like Sarah, Abraham's wife, like Ásíyih, daughter to Pharaoh, like Mary the Virgin, and
Fáṭimih, our Lady of Light, and the freshly-
martyred Ṭáhirih, from the Dispensation of the
Báb.

'How sweet', Bahá'u'lláh addressed her, 'thy
presence . . . how sweet . . . to make mention
of thee . . .'[5]

And when He was under terrible attack from
mortal enemies both within and without the
Faith, 'Abdu'l-Bahá wrote to tell her that some
day they would be together in the life to come,
'beneath the sheltering shadow of the Blessed
Beauty', and would think no more of their
agonies on earth. And He said on that day every
one of the calumnies that had been spread so far
and wide would all be made up for by the praise
and favour of Bahá'u'lláh. Again He wrote her,

3

'I can never, never forget thee.' And again, to
His daughter, he wrote of Khánum's life:
'Moth-like she circled in adoration round the
undying flame of the Divine Candle, her spirit
ablaze and her heart consumed . . .'[6]

After 1892, when Bahá'u'lláh passed away,
she was the one who stood by her Brother, the
appointed Centre of the Faith. By then her great
mother and her powerful uncle, Áqáy-i-Kalím,
were both gone. Her younger brother, praying
one twilight on the roof, had fallen through an
open skylight to his death in the prison.
'Abdu'l-Bahá's sons had not lived to grow up.
Barring Khánum, all He had for helpers then
were His consort and four unmarried daughters
– and one remembers how small a role was
possible for most women in that day and place,
especially women who were prisoners and
exiles.

The Master was now 'Forsaken, betrayed,
assaulted by almost the entire body of His relatives . . .'[7] He stood virtually undefended, at
bay; left by Himself to bear, let alone His shat-
tering grief, His terrible new burden: responsibility for the Cause of God. Meanwhile His
own kindred gathered and plotted against Him
in the Mansion of Bahjí and the houses round

about. From here, led by the murderous half-brother who coveted the headship of our Faith, they sent out missives and deputies across the Eastern world to vilify 'Abdu'l-Bahá. To His royal gaoler the Sultán, the paranoid 'Abdu'l-Ḥamíd, they denounced the captive Master as a rebel who was building a fortress on Mount Carmel and mobilizing an army to take over Turkish lands. We have only to read 'Abdu'l-Bahá's Will and Testament – which is like a personal letter from Him to each new believer down the centuries, sharing what He had kept concealed so long – to know what went on during that massive, concerted attack when they set the axe to the root of our Faith. 'Should they be suffered to continue,' He warned us during those years, 'they would, in but a few days' time, exterminate the Cause of God, His Word, and themselves.'[8]

'Abdu'l-Bahá's consort and His daughters (He had no sons-in-law then) helped as they could, but His one great champion at that time of the 'fierce onslaught of the forces of disruption' after 1892, of the unceasing, telling, diabolical manoeuvrings of their half-brother (which gave rise to threats and rumours that 'Abdu'l-Bahá would soon be banished to the

Fezzan, or hanged, or drowned), was His sister,
Bahíyyih.

When, as a result of that assault by His
kindred, 'Abdu'l-Ḥamíd reimposed a strict
incarceration on the Master, He was not set free
until the Revolution of the Young Turks
(1908), at which time the Sulṭán himself was
gaoled. The Master commented in after-years
that the chains were taken off His neck and
placed on 'Abdu'l-Ḥamíd's. He added that He
had been happy as a prisoner because He knew
He was suffering in the path of God, but that
this was not the case with 'Abdu'l-Ḥamíd,
imprisoned for his own deeds.[9]

A strange caricature of the despot was spread
in France around that time, showing him with
smoke curling about his head, the smoke
peopled with the faces of young women, and
underneath, a mocking caption that said: 'One
sweet consolation remains to him.' He died in
1918.

As soon as the Master was physically able
(illness turned Him back the first time He
started out) to promulgate the cause of global
peace, He departed on His historic teaching
journeys to the West, leaving His sister in
charge at the World Centre. Her great joy then

was to receive the accounts of spiritual victories that He won for the Faith in Europe and the new world. Those long, exhausting journeys during which – unlike every visitor representing any other faith we can call to mind – He paid His own way and accepted no funds, used up the last of His strength.

Then came the Great War. And all through those war years the famished, the destitute, the rejected, those held to be beneath consideration by their Ottoman Government, laid siege to the residence of 'Abdu'l-Bahá, and <u>Kh</u>ánum tended them. She fed them, gave them money and clothes, and doctored them with medicines invented through some process of her own.

As she reached old age, instead of retiring into harshness, or apathy, or self-indulgence, she grew ever more loving and serving. But then came the last, unbearable blow: in 1921, the loss of 'Abdu'l-Bahá.

She was getting on toward eighty then, but she began what was in effect a new career, as the one powerful champion of her grandnephew, Shoghi Effendi, now Guardian of the Faith. This was a time when, unforeseen by him and the Bahá'í world, 'Abdu'l-Bahá's Will had set on his young shoulders nothing less than the

7

annihilating burden of responsibility for the Cause of Bahá'u'lláh. During those early years of his illness and distress, she was, at least three times, in effect Regent of the Faith.

After she was gone he wrote that she had been his 'sole earthly sustainer', the 'joy and solace' of his life.[10] In a memorable tribute, he called her days to mind; wrote of the tenderness of her heart, her resignation and serenity which made him think of the Báb, her attraction to flowers and children, her 'unaffected simplicity', her 'undiscriminating' love and 'forgiving nature . . .' Again he recalled her 'unfailing solicitude . . . in the most critical and agitated hours of my life . . .' He would remember, he told her, the sweet magic of her voice, the touch of her hand, through all his darkest hours.[11]

As a young pilgrim I thought that everything in the Haifa Household was plain and unadorned. For comparisons you could say the rooms were in no way like Versailles, or the old Persian embassy in Stamboul, or the <u>Sh</u>áh's palace, its salon all crystal chandeliers, the walls set with thousands of bits of mirrors in floral designs, that would come alive and twinkle like diamonds when anyone passed by. I had, too, sometimes wandered through the sumptuous, great, lonely, left-over palaces, built and then quit, in the countryside north of Ṭihrán, mocking in their emptiness and decay the old-time Qájár dynasty's omnipotence, left now to a caretaker or so, huddled with his family in some abandoned room. There was nothing of all that in the simple Haifa homes.

We had come in a Dodge touring car, over the deserts from Ṭihrán, with the Nairn Company convoy; I believe we were the first pilgrims from Írán's capital to make the trip with such speed – seven days. We had left in secrecy, for in the same convoy was the American oilman who had escaped with his life when the diplomat, Imbrie, was assaulted by a mob near a Muslim shrine: they had followed him then to a hospital and murdered him in his bed.

On the floor-flat desert our driver, racing the herd, had shot a gazelle, and bundled it, the legs stiff, the great eyes dusted over, on the running-board of the car. We had come through the apricot-coloured ruins of Palmyra, Zenobia's city, and slept there, fleas and all, in a native house. As we drove south along the Mediterranean, and the Mansion of Bahjí appeared in the distance, my father rose and bowed from his seat in the Dodge.

He had been a young man in 1899, my father, a Persian who knew English, rare in those days when French was Persia's preferred Western tongue – and had run away from home and fled to the Master in 'Akká.

The journey took him months: he had come via Bákú, waited for permission in the Caucasus, crossed the Black Sea and come through Constantinople, travelled steerage, known hunger, and at last when he was brought into the Master's presence, he fainted away; the only portrait he had ever seen of 'Abdu'l-Bahá was the youthful photograph taken in Adrianople, and he thought he was seeing Bahá'u'lláh, now gone seven years.

They revived him with tea in an adjoining room, brought him back to 'Abdu'l-Bahá, and among the Master's opening remarks was the statement that the Cause of God had reached America, and that Father's knowing English would be of use. The Master then handed him a pile of Tablets to translate. Father looked them over and panicked. 'But these are Arabic!' he said. The Master told him never mind, and gave him a handful of rock candy wrapped in a cloth, and told him Arabic would become as easy for him to translate as Persian.

From then on he had served 'Abdu'l-Bahá as amanuensis, virtually day and night, for over a year. And in 1901, much to his distress, he was sent by the Master to a place as far away as the moon – the new world, the other hemisphere, way across the vast, dark water that surrounds the earth – to serve as interpreter to the renowned Bahá'í philosopher Mírzá Abu'l-Faḍl.

In that frightening place, he found a bride, and a home. And so far as the records indicate, my parents next came as pilgrims to the Holy Land in 1906. Then, in 1912, they were able to serve 'Abdu'l-Bahá during His American journeys. The last time they ever saw Him was that day on the *Celtic* in New York harbour, that December 5, when Father translated the Master's parting words to the American Bahá'ís,[12] and now it was not without anguish that they neared 'Akká and Haifa, where they had once been in 'Abdu'l-Bahá's presence, and could be no more.

Father was away from the family when we lost 'Abdu'l-Bahá. Dramatically enough, he was conducting the Crown Princess of Persia, Mahín-Bánú, and her party the long way round, via India, back to Ṭihrán so that she could there give birth to the future Qájár Sháh. On that journey he was surrounded by Muslims at all times; but all along, wherever his ship put into port, weeping groups of believers would come on board to be with him. The endless days somehow went by, and the Princess' time was running out. At one point in Persia, in heavy snow, Father had to have five hundred men clear a road up one side of a mountain, and five hundred clear the other side down. A few days after they arrived in Ṭihrán, so did the infant: a girl.

We two sisters and our mother were living in a rented house at Stenia, up the Bosporus, then, and later in a Pera hotel, as the winter shut down. By early spring we set out, attended by Father's Muslim secretary, Javád Khán Vuthúq, across the Black Sea, by way of Bákú and the Caspian, followed by wearying days in an open car, across a moonscape to Ṭihrán. Our mother brought with her a precious charge which had been entrusted to her by the Bahá'ís of Constantinople, and carefully concealed: the first copy of the Master's Will to reach Írán. The believers in the Ḥaẓíratu'l-Quds at Bákú, assisted by Javád <u>Kh</u>án, sat up deep into the night, each one copying out a different section of the Will until the task was done.

When, on his journey, Father learned of Shoghi Effendi's appointment (for <u>Kh</u>ánum had cabled the Bahá'í world), he wrote a letter to Mother, saying that if 'Abdu'l-Bahá had told him to bow down before a stone, he would have bowed down before that stone, and here the Master had given us this glorious and youthful Being for our protector and guide.

Always, he had spoken of the Household with reservations. 'The Household is not the Master,' he would say, referring to the men of the Family, since the ladies, according to the custom of that day, lived in seclusion. The only exception Father made was with regard to Shoghi Effendi, when the Guardian-to-be visited with our family many times during his months in France. 'Like a small diamond cut from a large diamond,' Father said. 'All the qualities.'

Towards the Guardian he was, as the French might have it, more royalist than the king. One day on this present pilgrimage he came back from his walk with the Guardian along Mount

Carmel. 'Today,' he said, 'the Guardian stopped at a certain spot in the road and explained to me that he is entirely different from 'Abdu'l-Bahá. It was the same spot in the road where the Master once stopped, and explained to me that He was entirely different from Bahá'u'lláh.'

We had often been in Shoghi Effendi's presence when he was in Paris on his way to Oxford, but now for the first time we were to visit him as Guardian, as the one 'blest and sacred', the 'chosen branch', the 'expounder', the one to be obeyed by all of us and to obey none, the 'sign of God (*Áyatu'lláh*)' – of 'Abdu'l-Bahá's Will. It was a very sensitive time in the history of our Faith. All would be new and strange.

How can one hope to describe Khánum? Only now, reading her writings, do I perceive a glimmer of what the world lost when, almost fifty years ago, she unobtrusively took her leave.

Bahá'ís world-wide mourned her a full nine months; but probably we thought only, as most people would, that a fragile lady, advanced in years and at the last confined to her bed, had after a long life of continual service, passed to

glory. Yet the Guardian wrote that for human-
ity, the loss of her was 'irreparable'.[13]

Trying to visualize her now by her opposite,
I imagine the stereotype of a lady 'chairperson'
of the Occident, complete with glasses, ear-
rings, neck chains and lapel brooch, presiding
over a club of similar ladies who have come to
the meeting for the purpose of planning their
next meeting – and gavelling them down.

No, all I can find to say is that she was a
quietness, a focal point of peace; that she per-
vaded the room like a sweet scent, or lit her
corner like a sun-ray shining through a crystal
vase; that despite her rank and great dignity, she
was self-effacing, gentle-voiced; and that she
spoke little, but you remembered.

The Ladies of 'Abdu'l-Bahá's Household wore
very plain garments, although crisp and fresh,
and each covered her head with the Persian
chárqad, a large white kerchief that fastened
under the chin and spread over breast and
shoulders. Even in Ṭáhirih's day something like
this head-dress was the rule. For married
women in Persia, well into this century, the hair
would be cut in bangs and worn short about the

ears. Then in back, hidden under the kerchief, there would be many tiny braids, dark brown and with reddish henna gleams. In the Haifa Household, however, the ladies did not wear the bangs and curls; their foreheads were unadorned.

For the married women of the Middle East, there had always been cosmetics, as there always have been (a circumstance due, of course, not to the vanity of women, but the gullibility of men). I saw the old style make-up in Persia, the face almost, it seemed, enamelled, the dark brows joined, or with a vertical dark hair-line between. The mouth, for beauty, had to be small, virtually invisible, the poets liked to say, and it was not emphasized. It was a rose unopened, the poets said; or in laughter, a rose blossoming. And there might be a beauty spot beside it – likened by poets to many things, such as the grain in a trap for the bird of a man's heart, or to a little black boy sitting by a well, in which case the well would be the dimple in the chin.

The Guardian told us that Ṭáhirih's beauty differed from Western concepts of beauty. It is pretty certain, however, that she used cosmetics. She must have, the day she cast aside the _chádur_ and unveiled her face at Bada_sh_t: at least, the text says she was 'adorned', and she was a very feminine individual; we also find two or three references to her clothes, although the Master says that 'she never cared for dress'.[14] (Those who stand for women's rights might like to know that Írán's Ṭáhirih, poet and schol-ar, declared those rights at Bada_sh_t _before_ the famous American gathering, met for the same purpose, at the home of Elizabeth Cady Stan-ton, 19 July 1848 – and that Ṭáhirih went on to become 'the first woman suffrage martyr'.[15])

We gather from a poem of hers that she also had the tiny black beauty spot, as well as curling locks to either side of her face, as seen in the portrait of a lady in _The Dawn-Breakers_[16] – for she writes:

Beside the lip one beauty spot,
And yet these curling locks are twain;
Sad the heart's bird, sad its lot:
Two snares, and but a single grain.

But in Haifa, there was not much in the way of cosmetics, except that the ladies of the Household, the married ones, following local custom, used a tiny line of kohl around the eyes, particularly the lower lids. This was fetching, even for the elderly. The Master's consort,

Munírih <u>Kh</u>ánum, was a handsome aged lady when we saw her. She was, through her great-grandmother, descended from a princess of an Indian royal house, while her father's descent was from the Prophet Muḥammad. She had a delightful, slightly arched nose, and her presence was aristocratic, in the sense of being gracious and at ease. Her skin was the colour of mellowed white lace, and she wore the little eye-line of kohl.

<u>Kh</u>ánum, however, used no make-up of any kind. For one thing, that was for the married, and she had dedicated her entire life to the Faith. She never considered marriage at all, away from her task.

In those days Carmel, the ancient Mountain of God, was mostly ragged – all weeds and rocks, but following 'Abdu'l-Bahá, the Guardian had continued with its embellishment. The fruit trees were already there, and there was a rich patch of green grass which Shoghi Effendi specially pointed out to Mother, taking her arm one night to guide her over the uneven ground. Walking back of them I wished I were old, so that he would take my arm too. There above us were Curtis Kelsey's electric lights on the (domeless) Shrine of the Báb itself, thrusting brightly down the mountain – the very lights Curtis had been installing at the time of the Master's passing. The great beam cut down through the night, making a golden path through the dark, and it was teeming with thousands of bugs, every kind, flown in from the night, and in after-years these seemed to me a symbol of the believers, dark before they entered the Faith, now willy-nilly, worthy or not worthy, turned to gold. The light shimmered on the low, polished leaves of the palms the Guardian had recently planted to line the straight, steep path from the German Colony at the mountain's foot, up to the Shrine. Here was an old, worn-away mountainside, mostly barren ground and rubble; yet the Guardian turned to Mother and said (I admit to my surprise): 'It has not yet achieved the grandeur of Versailles.'

When Shoghi Effendi was in Paris on his way to Oxford, Mother had arranged a picnic for him at Versailles, and Chaybani, Father's secretary, had escorted him there. It is probable that without Shoghi Effendi's vision as to the future of our Faith, then little known in the world, many of the believers of that time – after their devastating loss of 'Abdu'l-Bahá – would not have had the courage to keep on. The Guardian inspired the believers with his own certitude, and when they left him, they were on fire to serve. It used to remind me of Napoleon's dictum that an army of deer headed by a lion is better than an army of lions headed by a deer.

On this first pilgrimage of mine, the third anniversary of the Master's passing came due. The wound was raw, and there was a great outburst of Eastern grief: tears, loud cries and sobs; and seeing the adults in disarray, the children began whimpering and running about, not knowing where to turn. The house was full of people, and the sounds of weeping were all about, when I happened to walk by the open doorway of a lighted room, and there, through the door, was the Greatest Holy Leaf. She was seated in the midst of the children, they standing close to her as if all were in her embrace; she still and quiet, sitting there detached from the storm, her face composed, a comfort and safe haven.

I also have a memory of climbing up Mount Carmel that night under great crystal chandeliers of stars, and Dr Esslemont pausing in the climb, probably for breath (he would live less than a year from then), and saying, 'The heavens declare the Glory of God, and the firmament showeth His handiwork'. Esslemont was slight and fair, quiet, low-key, with an admirable sense of humour, and we felt much drawn to him. He was studying Persian and Arabic in those days. I remember that on another occasion, near Bahjí, he quoted a verse to me about Muḥammad and the First Imám, 'Alí:

To our Master 'Alí said the Prophet of God:
'Scourge thy body with a rod.'

However, because of the word-play, the verse could also be read thus:

The Prophet of God bade our Master 'Alí:
'O slothful be, O slothful be.'

(*Guft Payqambar bá Mawláná 'Alí: Tan balí kun, tan balí kun, tan balí.*)

The display of grief that night had been inordinate, and the Guardian reportedly commented that service to the Faith would be preferable to the cries and tears. He himself was always most contained and dignified. We were told that after he had lost Khánum, he attended one of the memorial meetings and as he sat there the tears poured down his face, but he ignored them. This reserve in such circumstances is un-Persian, it is of the West – but then, we are not committed to this behaviour pattern or the other. I once heard him say of us all: 'We are neither Eastern nor Western, we are Bahá'ís.'

I did not understand what was going on beneath what was going on that night, but my Persian father knew. Here was the young Guardian, new in the successorship, and here, from the relatives, was the ostentation, the 'bravery' of all this grief: a genuine emotion, certainly, but also being used. Later many of those faithless weepers would take themselves off, or their children would, as the Guardian's future cables, heart-breaking in their restraint, would tell the Bahá'í world. He writes in *God Passes By*[17] that the rebellion of Mírzá Muḥammad-'Alí, half-brother of 'Abdu'l-Bahá, against the Master in 1892 – when Bahá'u'lláh left this world – had 'sealed ultimately the fate of the great majority' of Bahá'u'lláh's family members. What they were now saying with their tears and moans was: 'See what we have lost!'

Father soon afterward asked for an audience

with the ladies of the Household, in his capacity
as a one-time Secretary of 'Abdu'l-Bahá, who
had lived in the Master's presence so long, and
had been known to them so many years. They
came together to hear him, and he addressed
them as protocol required, seated outside a
partially-opened door.

Whether Khánum was in their midst, I do not
know; in any case, his remarks were not addressed to her. The Master's consort was present.
We knew at first hand of her heavy affliction,
for she had commented to our family, compar-
ing 'Abdu'l-Bahá and the Guardian, her eyes,
that had looked on death so often before this
worst goodbye of all, raised to Heaven: 'This
one a drop, that One a sea.' (*Ín qaṭrih, án daryá.*)
Understandable words, when we remember
that after all the Master was her husband, the
Guardian was her grandson, and her Beloved
was gone; but words that would not have been
uttered by Khánum of her youthful grandnephew, whose station as conferred by the Will
her writings show that she clearly knew. Not
that anyone would have compared his rank to
that of the matchless Mystery of God: but the
Guardian was the sacred 'sign of God', the
'Dayspring of Divine Guidance', the Will says,

and all were to be lowly before him.

What Father told them that morning, through the crack in the door, was that expressions of loud despair were no way to rally about the Guardian in obedience to the Will, no way to thank 'Abdu'l-Bahá for seeing to it that we were not left orphaned.

What particularly remains in memory about Khánum is her quiet, brief sentences, voiced as if in confidence and shared with you as a friend. I was a person inclined to brood and ponder, like on those autumn evenings in the circular entrance hall of the Master's house, when a strange blue light would come shedding from the darkening sky. There were two American girls on pilgrimage then, and I – so many years in Europe and the East – was surprised to find they were not unhappy too. I asked if they had good times. 'Never had anything else,' was the answer.

Once I said to Khánum, 'There is no happi-. ness in the world.' And she softly replied: 'Except in service to the Cause of God.' (*Magar khidmat bih Amru'lláh*).

There was a great homeyness about her.

Once when I was sitting by her in what was called the Tea Room – a rather long room with plain, unadorned divans all along the walls – some American ladies came in (Marjorie Morten, I think, with Mrs Mountfort Mills) and they had their hats on. The Greatest Holy Leaf leaned over and confided to me: 'The hats make them ugly' (*Kuláh zishtishún míkunih*). Among the visitors was a widow from the Middle East, who had arrived on what seemed to be a permanent pilgrimage. I do not recall the source of this lady's equally permanent melancholy. True, she would help some of the people there on occasion, sitting on the floor according to lingering custom and working on the vegetables and other ingredients of the patriarchal dinner dishes that would feed so many mouths. But she would take little part in the conversations, being mostly wrapped in unadulterated grief. One day, there she came, and sat, heaving her usual sighs, her face clouded with sorrow. Gently, the Greatest Holy Leaf leaned over and addressed her. 'There are no frontiers to the world of gloom,' she said (*'álam-i-khíyál*). 'You will never get to the end of it, no matter how far and how fast you gallop your steed.'

Khánum could be strict. We heard some

complaints from Mírzá Yaḥyá's granddaughter, for instance. Mírzá Yaḥyá, unrelenting foe
of his half-brother, Bahá'u'lláh, and who, from
envy, had repeatedly attempted to murder the
Manifestation of God – the granddaughter of
such a man was now being cared for in the
Household of the Guardian. Life there was too
strict, she said, she could not go to the cinema.
The exiled Family were, after all, living under
continual scrutiny, and had carefully to observe
the proprieties of the time and place.

Again, I recall Khánum's displeasure with a
young girl who kissed her hand; this obsequi-
ousness is forbidden in the Aqdas. Munírih
Khánum Ayádí (the daughter of one Hand of
the Faith and wife of another) once told me that
when her two little boys were in the Master's
presence and bowed low, in the Persian fashion,
the Master said: 'No. Like this' – and, His back
straight, He saluted. Hand kissing in the family,
to show affection, was not forbidden; but He
made it clear that the long millennia of bowing,
scraping, and tugging at the forelock, are gone
at last.

One's fellow-believers in general are apt to be
very specific about what is called, mysteriously

enough, the 'foreseeable future'. With no sup-
porting Bahá'í text, they lay down the law
about what is going to transpire. And yet the
history of our Faith is full of surprises,
developments undreamt of by the average
believers of any given day: looking back, I see
that time and again, they have, albeit most sin-
cerely, told me wrong. It is unsafe to put one's
foot down and say, categorically, with no
authority, this will happen, or this will not
happen.

At a time when no one else knew what was
planned for the Faith after the Master, no one
else including Shoghi Effendi himself, the Most
Exalted Leaf was entrusted with the secret. It
was a time when no one had heard the word
'Guardian' in its Bahá'í sense. A time when any
believer would have told you that after
'Abdu'l-Bahá, there would be the House of Justice: the House of Justice would then be established. Established on what, asks Rúḥíyyih
Khánum, in her appraisal of those days.[18]

But strangely enough, to one other individual, this one not a member of the Bahá'í
Faith, the secret of 'Abdu'l-Bahá's successor
was also disclosed. This woman became a
believer in after years, and wrote her story for

the German Bahá'í national publication, *Sonne der Wahrheit*.[19] Her name was Dr Fallscheer, but she was known by the title Ḥakímih, Lady Doctor.

One summer day – it was 6 August 1910 – when the doctor got home from a professional call, she received this message, brought by a servant of 'Abbás Effendi, 'Abdu'l-Bahá: Would Ḥakímih come that afternoon to the Ḥaramlik, the Ladies' Household, because one of the serving-women had a badly infected finger.

The doctor was tired. It was hot, and besides, this was a Saturday, her day off. But she knew that 'Abdu'l-Bahá would never have sent for her unless the need was urgent. She was already familiar with the case. For weeks she had tried to get the little maid, Farídih, to let her lance the finger – but at the very thought of it, Farídih would only clap her hands to her ears and scream; she much preferred her own remedy, a poultice of onions, tomatoes, and a species of cactus. Finally, 'Abdu'l-Bahá insisted that the maid be properly attended to.

We should add here that Western ideas about a staff of servants would be far off the mark. Here were poor people, being fed, clothed, and cared for, working about the house just as did the family. There were no social services to fall back on, the direst poverty was only a stone's throw away, and a kind of patriarchal system was what kept them living. Such an account as Myron H. Phelps's book, *Abbas Effendi, His Life and Teachings*, makes this clear.

Ḥakímih went, lanced the finger, all was well, and the Greatest Holy Leaf sent the little girl off to bed. Khánum then invited the doctor for coffee with the ladies of the Household. They sat, chatting over the coffee cups, their conversation in Turkish, which the doctor knew better than Arabic. (Some two years later, in New York, the Master told inventor Hudson Maxim: 'I also speak Turkish and Arabic; Turkish is very difficult. In the East it is thought that acquiring Turkish is equivalent to the study of three other tongues.'[20]) Khánum herself was well versed in Turkish, Persian and Arabic.

An attendant then appeared and asked Ḥakímih to come and see 'Abdu'l-Bahá in the reception room before she left. Accordingly, Khánum led her up an inner stair to the floor above, to the reception room at the left of the main entrance.

The Master asked Ḥakímih to report on her

little patient, and whether the danger of blood poisoning was over. His son-in-law, Mírzá Hádí, a tall, imposing man, came in to take his leave. Back of him the doctor suddenly noticed a child, 'Abdu'l-Bahá's eldest grandson, who entered and kissed the Master's hand. She had seen Shoghi Effendi a number of times before, but only casually; and just recently, Khánum had confided to the doctor that this child, the eldest in the direct line, had been 'designated as the coming successor or Vizier of the Master'.

While his Grandfather and father conversed, young Shoghi Effendi greeted the ladies, and then waited respectfully near the door. (The door in many Eastern countries is the 'lower' part of the room. Here is the 'shoe-row', where, traditionally, shoes are left on entering. Here the attendants may wait. The point farthest from the 'shoe-row' is the 'highest' part of the room.) Several Persian gentlemen then entered the room, and about a quarter of an hour was 'spent in leave-takings and in greetings', and comings and goings.

During this interval Khánum and the doctor retired to the window-seat on the upper right-hand side of the reception room, and conversed in Turkish. The doctor, meanwhile, never took her eyes off the child, who was dressed in a European summer suit – a short jacket and short trousers but with long stockings reaching above the knee. He seemed to be eleven or twelve, she later wrote, and what struck her in the young face was 'the dark, early advanced, yes even melancholy eyes'. The boy stood motionless 'in his respectful, expectant bearing and posture'. Then, the room emptying, he slowly approached his beloved Grandfather and waited for Him to speak, then replied diffidently in Persian, then was dismissed with a smile and, not permitted this time to kiss the Master's hand, backed respectfully out of the room, all the time, Ḥakímih writes, keeping 'his dark, true-hearted eyes steadily on the blue, magic glances of his Grandfather'.

(After reading many accounts, we believe both the Master and the Guardian must have had hazel eyes. My father, with Him well over a year, so described the eyes of 'Abdu'l-Bahá: they would vary in colour, he said. And one day in Haifa, when sky and sea were bright blue, we saw the Guardian standing under the Bougainvillaea vine at the gate to 'Abdu'l-Bahá's house, and on that day his eyes were bright blue.)

Then, as 'Abdu'l-Bahá approached them, the

31

ladies rose. He told them to resume their seats and Himself reclined on an ottoman beside them.

'Now my daughter,' He said, 'how do you like Shoghi Effendi, my Elisha to be?'

His reference, adds the doctor, was to II Kings 2:13. Elisha was the successor to Elijah, and the Bible says: 'The spirit of Elijah doth rest on Elisha'.

Here was Ḥakímih's strange reply: 'Master, if I am permitted to speak, I must state that in his boyish countenance are the eyes of a sufferer, who is to suffer greatly.' (We have a photograph of Shoghi Effendi taken just about that time. The photographer in Berkeley, California, who copied it remarked: 'As the Germans say, *Wunderaugen* . . .')

She goes on to comment that 'Abdu'l-Bahá then looked over their heads, far off into the distance. Then He told her: 'My grandson's eyes are not the eyes of one who "prepares the way"; they are not a fighter's eyes, not a victor's eyes – but there is in his gaze a depth of loyalty, of perseverance, of conscientiousness. And do you know, my daughter, why he was destined for this difficult heritage as my Vizier, the fulfiller of my duties?'

Continuing, His gaze fixed more intently on the Greatest Holy Leaf, He said: 'Bahá'u'lláh, blessed are His words now and forevermore, appointed this trifling individual, myself, as His successor, not because I was the first-born, but because His inner sight recognized, even years before, the sign of God on my forehead. Before His departure into the Eternal Light, He reminded me that I, at some time, and without regard to birthright or age, would have to look to my sons and even grandsons, to see whom God would choose to be my heir. My sons left this world at a tender age, and among all my kin and blood relatives only little Shoghi has the shadow of a great calling in the depth of his eyes.' Then a long pause. And then He said: 'At this time, the British world empire is the greatest of all and is still advancing. Its language is a world language. My Vizier shall receive his education in England itself, after acquiring the Oriental languages and the wisdom of the East in this place.'

The doctor ventured to object: Would not Western education 'check his active spirit', rigidly bind it, 'stifle his Oriental non-rationalities and intuition into dogmas and conventionalities,' so that he would turn away from being a servant of the Most High and become 'a slave of Western opportunism and the trite and commonplace'?

A long pause. Then 'Abdu'l-Bahá stood up and said in a firm voice, 'I am not giving my Elisha to the British for education: I am consecrating him to Almighty God. May His eyes watch over my child . . . even at Oxford.'

With no further word or gesture, the Master left the room. The doctor took leave of Khánum, and as she went, observed 'Abdu'l-Bahá in His garden, lost in deep thought, examining a fruit-bearing fig tree.

In November 1921, when Ḥakímih was living in Lugano, she learned of the passing of 'Abdu'l-Bahá, and her thoughts turned back to that August in 1910, and she wished that all things good would befall 'Elisha Shoghi'. Her account ends: 'Inshá'alláh!'

Dr Fallscheer became a Bahá'í upon her return to Germany, and not long before she died. When Dr Hermann Grossmann, Hand of the Cause, and his wife Anna, asked the Guardian about these notes, Shoghi Effendi replied that the Master 'must have had great confidence in Dr Fallscheer, since, at a time when He may have first considered sending Shoghi Effendi to

England, He told her of it, and on the same occasion said that Shoghi Effendi was to be His "Vizier".'[21]

On our pilgrimage, there was also the evening of the rings. About half a dozen girls were visiting that evening, in 'Abdu'l-Bahá's house, when Khánum, in the simplest way, hardly even noticeably, distributed a Bahá'í ring to each.

Many things would happen to us all with the years, and it is probable that most of those rings are gone now, and most of the recipients as well. I know the two Americans with all the good times are gone now, that they went young, that their slim fingers are gone, let alone their rings. The others also met their various fates, and this ring of mine is probably the only one left from that evening of the rings. It is an oblong, dark green stone, chrysoprase, I think, from the deserts in the Holy Land. These are delicate stones; an end chipped off, and a jeweller filled it in with gold; also, its carving is now worn and blurred. But it is the same stone that Khánum gave me that night.

It would be good in this place to mention two more memories of the Greatest Holy Leaf, one by Martha Root, the 'star-servant', and our century's 'foremost Hand',[22] the other by beautiful Juliet the artist, whom 'Abdu'l-Bahá said the queens would envy in days to come.

Here is Martha's, from a talk she gave in Vienna, 29 January 1933, when she told her Bahá'í audience: 'The Greatest Holy Leaf has said that if, after death, she should be found worthy to enter the presence of her Father, the first thing she would ask of Him would be His help for His toiling followers.'

And here is Juliet's, from her diary, written 18 August 1909:

Day before yesterday, in the blessed company of Khánum and the Holy Mother, we climbed Mount Carmel to the Holy Tomb and the Carmelite Monastery. We went into the chapel of the Monastery. On the altar, surrounded by candles, sat the Madonna, a crudely carved wooden doll – life-size – with a scarlet spot painted on each cheek and draped in jewels and satin. From a rose-window high in the opposite wall – a win-

dow that faced 'Akká – rays streamed to a
pool of light on the floor. Then in marched
the brown-robed monks and knelt in the
pool of light, their backs turned to 'Akká,
their bowed heads to the altar. The rays
poured on their backs as they prayed to the
wooden doll. My thoughts were running on
this, *condemning* the monks, when <u>Kh</u>ánum
slipped her arm through mine.

'It is good,' she whispered, 'to be here
together in a place built for worship.'

Later, in the Cave of Elijah, I saw her standing by the altar there, that wonderful face,
second only to the Master's, raised to the
crucifix; her eyes lowered once or twice to
the image of the Virgin prostrate beneath it.
Ah, well could *she* understand such suffering.
My tears flowed as I watched her.

She was, the Guardian told us, united by a 'mystic
bond' with the spirit of her Father; and again, she
was linked closely with her Brother, 'Abdu'l-
Bahá, 'the perfect Exemplar of that Spirit'. She
was the Holy Household's 'most precious great
Adorning'.[23] These are amazing statements to be
made of a woman, in history's light, and typical
of the new age in which we live.

Yes, she is gone from the earth, but it is sweet to dwell on the memory of her – now that, in some world that we understand nothing about, she sings the words her Father gave her – sings out her 'love-song' on the Holy Tree. She, the Family's 'Adorning'; she, the 'beloved' of 'Abdu'l-Bahá's soul, and the 'joy and solace' of Shoghi Effendi's life; she, the 'last remnant' of Bahá'u'lláh, and the 'fragrance' of His 'shining robe'.[24]

REFERENCES

[1] Eight of the references for this essay are to *The Bahá'í World*, Vol. V (New York, 1936; reprinting Wilmette, 1981) – a section entitled 'The Passing of Bahíyyih K͟hánum, the Most Exalted Leaf'. The extracts are taken from a cablegram sent by Shoghi Effendi, the Guardian of the Bahá'í Faith, 15 July 1932, announcing the passing of Bahíyyih K͟hánum; passages from Tablets revealed by Bahá'u'lláh and 'Abdu'l-Bahá; and a Tribute penned by the Guardian on 17 July 1932. The reference will mention their source and give the page number in *Bahá'í World*. (The reader will find these documents reprinted in *A Compendium of Volumes of The Bahá'í World, I–XII* (Oxford, 1981), pp. 24–32.)
This first reference is to the Tribute, p. 175.
[2] Nabíl-i-A'zam, *The Dawn-Breakers* (Wilmette, 1932), dedication.
[3] See *The Bahá'í World*, Vol. V, pp. 174–5, Tribute.
[4] Shoghi Effendi, *God Passes By* (Wilmette, 1974), p. 347.
[5] *The Bahá'í World*, Vol. V, p. 171, passages from Tablets of Bahá'u'lláh.
[6] ibid. pp. 171–2, passages from Tablets of 'Abdu'l-Bahá.
[7] Shoghi Effendi, *God Passes By*, p. 247.
[8] 'Abdu'l-Bahá, *The Will and Testament of 'Abdu'l-Bahá*, various sources including *The Covenant of Bahá'u'lláh – A Compilation* (London, 1963), p. 114.

[9] See 'Abdu'l-Bahá, *The Promulgation of Universal Peace*, Vol. I (Chicago, 1921–2), p. 220.

[10] *The Bahá'í World*, Vol. V, p. 169, cablegram.

[11] ibid. pp. 179, 178, Tribute.

[12] See 'Abdu'l-Bahá, *The Promulgation of Universal Peace*, Vol. II (Chicago, 1925), pp. 464–7.

[13] Shoghi Effendi, *Messages to America* (Wilmette, 1947), p. 1.

[14] *Star of the West*, Vol. IV, No. 12, p. 210 (reprinted Oxford, 1978).

[15] Shoghi Effendi, *God Passes By*, p. 75.

[16] Nabíl-i-A'zam, *The Dawn-Breakers*, p. 624.

[17] Shoghi Effendi, *God Passes By*, p. 246.

[18] See *The Bahá'í World*, Vol. XI (Wilmette, 1952), p. 122. From 'Twenty-Five Years of the Guardianship'.

[19] Our present account is based on the English translation of the doctor's story by H. G. Paul, New York City, January 1931, copy in possession of the author.

[20] *Star of the West*, Vol. III, No. 7, p. 5 (reprinted Oxford, 1978).

[21] Copy of letter from Frau Anna Grossmann to Lili Olitzki Hermann, 5 June 1958, translated by Lili and Carl Hermann, in author's possession.

[22] Shoghi Effendi, *Messages to America*, pp. 39, 30.

[23] *The Bahá'í World*, Vol. V, p. 169, cablegram.

[24] ibid. pp. 171, 172, 169, passages from Tablets of Bahá'u'lláh and 'Abdu'l-Bahá, and cablegram.

www.ingramcontent.com/pod-product-compliance
Lightning Source LLC
Chambersburg PA
CBHW021227020426
42331CB00003B/505